William Davis

Job, and other poems

William Davis

Job, and other poems

ISBN/EAN: 9783337736934

Printed in Europe, USA, Canada, Australia, Japan

Cover: Foto ©ninafisch / pixelio.de

More available books at **www.hansebooks.com**

JOB

AND

OTHER POEMS.

BY

WILLIAM DAVIS.

CONTENTS.

	PAGE
JOB	3
On My Twenty-fifth Birthday	47
The Bells	49
To My Father	52
A Letter to Nannie	57
The Baron and His Typewritist	60
On Finding a Yellow Pup	64
An Incident	66
On the Naming of Hotel "Emory"	67
"Little William's" Thanks	68
A Simple Prayer	69
An Outcry	70
On the Birth of My Son	71
To W.—P.—B.	71
Satan's Song	75
My Poor Kitten	78
John Doodle's New Year's Resolution	81
To A Match	85
To ———	86
A Stanza	86
Impressions	87
On the Death of O. W. Holmes	88

CONTENTS.

An Enigmatical Valentine.	89
Lines on a Corpse	90
To My Parents.	92
Lines ———	96
To Georgie	96
The Valley of Rest	99
Truth	99
Night in a Graveyard	100
My Old Owl	101
Memory's Mission	103
To Duluth	105
Psalm XVIII (First Six Verses)	106
The Clocks	107
To Norfolk	108

JOB.

PART THE FIRST.

I.

In the land of Uz there dwelt a man—
An upright and God-fearing man—
An holy man, a perfect one;
Who sought the good to evil shun.
His name was Job, the one oppress'd;
Who, through his mis'ries, God confessed.
His wealth and power had so increased,
He was the greatest in the East.
Now seven sons to Job were born;
Three daughters did his home adorn.
His substance, too, had waxed so great
That Job could by the thousands rate
His household; which all told was eleven;
His sheep a thousand count by seven;
He had five hundred yoke of oxen;
His camels six times that had waxen.
To add to these enormous masses,
He had five hundred female asses.

And all his sons they went their way
And feasted, every one his day;
And also for their sisters sent;
And when the feasting days were spent,
Job rose up early in the morning

To offer off'rings burnt, according
To the number of them all—
And sanctified them each and all.
"And this," Job said, "Because it may
Be that my sons have sinned this day;
And in their hearts forgot to pray,
But cursed the God who set us free"—
And thus did Job continually.

II.

A day now was when the sons of God
Came to present, before the Lord,
Themselves; and Satan also came.
The Lord then said unto the same :
"Whence comest thou?" Then Satan said :
"To and fro in th' earth I tread."
And then these words the Lord delivered :
"Hast thou my servant Job considered,
That there's none like him in th' earth,
An upright, perfect man from birth,
And one that looks to God with fear,
And evil shuns, nor holds it dear?"
Then Satan summoned answ'ring thought,
And said: "Doth Job fear God for naught?
Hast thou not made an hedge around
About him and his house and ground;
And all he hath, on every side,
So him no evil may betide?
Thou, too, hast blest the work of his hand;
His substance is increased in the land.
But, now, on everything he hath,
(With seeming unrelenting wrath)

JOB.

On all, thy hand put forth and place,
And he will curse thee to thy face."
The Lord to Satan made reply :
"His all doth in your power lie;
But not 'pon him thy hand be spent."
So Satan from the Lord's presence went.

One day, while in their brother's house,
His sons and daughters did carouse,
A messenger to Job made haste,
And said: "My master, death I've faced—
And I, alone, escaped to tell,
The Sabeans 'pon the oxen fell,
And, with th' asses, took them 'way;
And slain the servants, too, have they."
While he was speaking yet, there came
Another one, and said : "The flame
Of God did from the heavens leap,
Consumed the servants and the sheep."
Another yet his story told :
"Chaldeans fell upon and stole
The camels, and the servants slew."
Before his message he was through,
Another came and did relate
How while his sons and daughters ate
And drank, a mighty wind came then
And smote the house and killed the men.

And so, from grief, arose up Job,
And shaved his head and rent his robe;
And said : "Oh naked was I born,
And naked thither shall return.

The Lord my riches gave—he came
And took them—blessed be his name."
In all this trial Job sinn'd not.
Nor charged his God,—nor cursed his lot.

III.

Before the Lord there came again
The sons of God; and to obtain
A presence, Satan also came.
The Lord then said unto the same :
"Whence comest thou?" Then Satan said :
"To and fro in th' earth I tread."
And then these words the Lord deliver'd :
"Hast thou my servant Job consider'd,
That there's none like him in the earth,
An upright, perfect man from birth,
And one that looks to God with fear,
And evils shuns nor holds it dear?
'Gainst him, for thee, myself I cast,
And still he holdeth to the last
His honesty. A righteous man."
And thus, then, Satan's answer ran :
"Skin for skin, yea man will give
The all he hath to let him live.
But 'pon *himself* thy hand thou place,
And he will curse thee to thy face."
Then unto Satan said the Lord :
"The right to thee I now accord
To further test—his life be spared."
So Satan unto Job repaired,
And smote with boils from sole to crown.
Then 'mong the ashes Job sat down.

JOB.

His wife then said : "Curse God and die."
Job answered her : "Doth it imply,
To whom God hath his goodness lent,
To him no evil will be sent?"

When Job's three friends of this evil heard,
They came to mourn and speak their word
Of comfort. Off afar they wept,
Because they knew him not; and kept
A silence seven days they sate,
Because they saw his grief was great.

IV.

Then after this Job cursed his day,
The night in which conceived he lay,
And life, with anguish now o'erspread.
Against his lot Job spake and said :
  "Let the brightness of the morn,
    And the night when I was born,
    Perish; darkness light dispel,
    And a cloud upon it dwell.
    God above his heed decline;
    Neither light upon it shine.
    Solitary be that night;
    Darkness take the place of light.
    Let therein no voice of joy;
    They that curse their curse employ.
    Let the twilight stars be dark,
    And no light within it lurk;
    For it gave unto me life,
    All this sorrow and this strife.

Why did me the knees prevent?
Why the birth I now lament?
Now I should have silent lain,
Rest and quiet sleep obtain.
Or, as an untimely birth,
I had never seen the earth.
Death, alone, can grant relief
To my mis'ry and my grief.
There the wicked ne'er molest—
There the weary be at rest—
There the pris'ners all rejoice—
There is heard no driver's voice—
There the small and great both be,
Servants from their masters free.
Why is light unto him given
Who with mis'ries' pangs is riven?
Why should life, beyond control,
Burden more the grievous soul,
Which for death doth long and crave,
And is glad to find the grave?
Why is not the light forbid
To a man whose way is hid?
For my sighings come and go,
And my wails like waters flow,
That which I did greatly dread,
And of which I was afraid,
Has at last upon me come.
To my woe I shall succumb.
I, no quiet piece did claim,
Neither rest—yet trouble came."

JOB.

PART THE SECOND.

I.

Then Eliphaz, the Temanite,
To Job, God's judgments, did recite:
" If we, with thee, commune, wilt thou be griev'd?
But who from speaking can withhold himself?
Behold, thou hast instructed many, and
Thou, too, the weak hast strengthened; and the falling
Thy words upheld, and strengthened feeble knees.
But now it is upon thee come; thou faintest;
It toucheth thee and thou art troubled. Is
Not this thy fear, thy confidence, thy hope,
And the uprightness of thy ways? Think—
Who *ever* perished, being innocent?
Or where the righteous *ever* were cut off?
E'en as I've seen—they that plow
And sow iniquity and wickedness,
The same they reap, and by the blast of God
They perish, by his anger are consumed.
Now secrectly to me was brought a thing
Of which mine ear received a little. From
The visions of the night, when deep sleep falls
On man, a fear and trembling came upon me,
Which made my bones to shake. Before mine eyes
A spirit passed—an image—it stood still,
And all was silence; then I heard a voice :
'Shall mortal man presume to be more just
Than God? Shall man be purer than his maker?
Behold, he trusteth not his servants, and
His angels charged with folly; how much less

In them that dwell in houses built of clay,
And dust, and which are crushed before the moth?'
If there be any that will answer thee,
Call now; but yet to which saint wilt thou look?
The foolish man is killed by wrath, and envy
Slays the silly one.   Afflictions come
Not from the dust nor trouble from the ground.
Yet man is unto trouble born alike
The sparks that upward fly.
                              I would seek God,
And unto him would I commit my cause.
He doeth great and marv'lous things;
He giveth rain unto the earth and fields;
And in their craftiness, the wise he taketh
So they meet with darkness in the day.
The poor he saveth from the mighty's hand.
Happy is the man whom God correcteth!
Despise ye not, therefore, the chastenings
Of th' Almighty; for he maketh sore
And bindeth up; he woundeth and his hands
Make whole.   He shall deliver thee from death,
And neither shalt thou be afraid of beasts.
At famine and destruction thou shalt laugh.
And thou shalt rest in peace and shalt not err.
And shalt know that thy seed shalt be great;
And like a shock of corn in season, thou
In a full age shalt die.   Lo, this it is
As we have searched it; know it for thy good."

Job said: "Oh that my grief were weighed,
And my misfortune with it laid;

JOB.

For then 'twould weigh more than the sand;
From grief no words can I command.
God doth 'gainst me his wrath array,
His poisoned arrows in me stay.
Oh that I might have my request;
That God would quiet my unrest.
That should it please him, me destroy;
Then comfort yet should I enjoy.
What is my strength that I should long?
Or end, that I should life prolong?
My strength is not the strength of stones,
Nor out of brass is made my bones.
To them that with afflictions bend,
Their friends their pity should extend.
My brethren, ye have dealt with me,
As brook and stream, deceitfully.
For nothing to me have ye shown;
Ye see and fear my casting down.
Did I the wish, to you, impart,
To give me of your substance part?
Did I beg you, in my extreme,
Me from the mighty's hand redeem?
But teach me and I'll hold my tongue;
Reveal the sin to which I've clung.
How forcible are words that move!
What doth your arguing reprove?
Attempt ye to alleviate
The sufferings of the desperate
With speeches which are as the wind?
Or to reprove with words unkind?
Ye overwhelm the fatherless;
Your friend, ye with reproofs distress.

Upon me look and be content—
My truth, to you be evident.
I pray you, therefore, now return;
My taste perverse things can discern.
Somewhere, within life's dreary span,
There warfare is on earth for man.
As hirelings look for their reward,
My rest by weary nights is barr'd.
And when I lay me down I say:
'Oh when will come the dawn of day?'
All night I toss me to and fro,
Till rays of light from darkness grow.
My flesh is clothed with worms and dust;
My skin doth sicken and disgust.
My days are as a shuttle—swift—
In which no hope do I uplift.
And as the wind, so is my life,
With evil, grief and sorrow rife.
The eye of him who hath me seen,
Shall see no more—to death I lean.
As clouds are vanished and consum'd
Man's life from death is ne'er resum'd.
To earth he shall return no more;
To him none will his place restore.
I'll not, therefore, my mouth refrain,
But in bitterness of soul complain.
For when I say, 'my bed shall please,
Or my complaint my couch shall ease,'
'Tis then thou scarest me with dreams;
My sleep with visions crowded seems.
So that my soul doth strangling choose,
And life for death would gladly lose.

I would not live alway—leave me,
For all my days are vanity.
Why dost thou 'pon me set thy heart?
And when wilt thou from me depart?
I've sinn'd; to thee what shall I do,
Oh thou Preserver? Why have you
Unto myself made me a burden?
Why dost thou not my erring pardon?
For in the dust now shall I sleep,
And thou my presence wilt not keep."

II.

To show God justice doth provide,
The Shuite, Bildad, then replied.
" How long wilt thou speak thus? How long wilt thou
Speak words which are as a strong wind? Doth God
His judgment or his justice e'er pervert?
If, for transgression, he hath cast away
Thy children; if thou wouldst seek betimes
Thy God, and to him make thy supplication;
If thou wert pure and upright; surely he
Would make thy habitation prosperous.
Though thy beginning small, thy latter end
Should greatly increase. Prepare thyself for search;
Enquire, I pray thee, of the *former* age,
(For we are but of yesterday, and know
Naught; because our days are as a shadow.)
Their fathers shall thee teach. The flag whilst green,
And not cut down, doth wither; so the paths
Of all that God forget. The hyp'crite's hope
Shall perish, and his house shall not endure.

God will not cast away a perfect man,
Nor will he help the evil-doers, till
He fill thy mouth with laughing, and thy lips
He, with rejoicing, fill.
And they that hate thee shall be clothed with shame;
The wicked's dwelling place shall come to naught."

Then Job to him his answer made:
"I know thou hast the truth portray'd.
But how shall man 'fore God be just?
Man cannot in contention trust
Himself with God; should he contend,
To answer man could not pretend.
In strength he's great, in heart he's wise;
His power man should realize.
Who ever hath against him set
Himself, and then with fortune met?
He turneth mountains from their base;
He shaketh th' earth from out its place;
The fiery path of Sun he bars—
It stops—he sealeth up the stars.
Alone, the heaven's sky he spreads;
Upon the waves of sea he treads;
He doeth great and wond'rous things;
And to their knees the proud he brings.
Then how shall I with him dispute?
For all I'd say he would confute.
Should he my call and voice receive,
That he replied, I'd not believe.
Around me doth his tempest rise;
My wounds by wounds he multiplies.

He will not let me take my breath,
But bitterness he gives till death.
In strength, his strength doth mine exceed,
In judgement, who shall say to plead?
Should my perfections I rehearse,
My own mouth would me prove perverse.
Though perfect I'd not know my soul,
'Gainst life my hate would I enrol.
No one, therefore, his life enjoys;
The good and wicked he destroys.
He gives the bad th' earth to rule,
And then the judges doth he fool.
My days are swifter than a flood—
They flee away, they see no good—
As swift as ships, they pass away—
As eagles hasten to their prey.
If my complaint I will suppress,
And will leave off my heaviness,
Thou wilt not hold me innocent:
If wicked, why then labor spent?
But he is not a man as I.
Let not his wrath me terrify,
Without a fear then would I speak.
But all's denied me that I seek.
My soul is cut off while I live;
I'll utterance to my sorrow give;
And say to God 'Do not condemn,
But show me why thou shouldst contemn.'
Shouldst thou thy handiwork despise?
Or seest thou with common eyes,
To find if wicked I have been,
As when thou searchest for my sin?

Before thee perfect now I stand,
And none can take from out thy hand.
My life, through thee, I did obtain—
Wilt thou bring me to dust again?
Remember, I beseech and pray,
That thou has made me as the clay.
Thou didst me life and favor grant
Thy spirit hath been vigilant.
These things within thy heart doth dwell;
Then why shouldst thou me now repel?
For if I sin thou markest me,
Nor pardon my iniquity.
Affliction with me doth increase ;
Thou takest from me all my peace.
Thy plagues against me are renewed—
I am with indignation viewed.
Why didst thou bring me from the womb?
Oh would they'd borne me to the tomb!
Leave me alone—my days are few—
That I my comfort may renew
Before I journey to that shore
Where death and darkness hover o'er:
That land of one eternal night—
That land in which there comes no light."

III.

Then Zophar, the Naamathite
Advises Job to be contrite:
"Should not the multitude of words be answer'd?
And should a man, who talks, be justified?
Should thy devices make men hold their peace?

And shall no man ashame thee when thou mockest?
For thou hast said that thou wert clean in sight
Of God; but oh that he would 'gainst thee speak,
And show thee wisdom's secrets; they are double
To that which is. Then know that God of thee,
Exacteth less than thou dost well deserve.
Canst thou by searching find out God? Canst thou
Find out and measure his perfection? It
Is high as heaven—so what canst thou do?
And deeper too, than hell—what canst thou know?
Then who can hinder him from cutting off?
He sees, and will consider, wickedness.
But vain man would be wise tho' born an ass.
If thou'lt prepare thine heart for him, and stretch
Thine hand toward him, and let no wickedness
Dwell in thy houses, and iniquity
Be put away from thee, then shalt thou
Lift up thy face, be steadfast and not fear.
Because thou shalt forget thy misery,
And think of it as waters passed away.
Thy age shall then be clean, and thou shalt shine.
And thou shalt be secure because there's hope.
In safety thou shalt take thy rest, and none
Shall frighten thee, but many look to thee.
The wicked's eyes shall fail and they shall not
Escape; their hope shall be as puffs of breath."

Then Job unto his three friends spake,
And to them did his answer make.
"No doubt but ye have sense, and wisdom too;
But I have understanding well as you.

With words, ye sought, my sorrow to appease—
But then, who knoweth not such things as these?
I am as one that's mocked and is forlorn—
The just and upright man is laughed to scorn.
He, who, with poverty, is agonized,
Is by the man of wealth and ease despised.
Prosperity with robbers doth endure;
And they that God provoke, he makes secure.
But ask the beasts and fowls, they shall thee teach
That God's hand doth thro' all creation reach.
He made all livings things in sea and land;
The life of all mankind is in his hand.
By days th' ancients wisdom did possess;
And God's omnipotence I now confess.
Behold, he shutteth up and breaketh down;
The earth he overturneth with his frown;
With him is strength and wisdom;—the deceiv'd,
By him, from the deceiver, is reliev'd.
The counsellors and judges doth he spoil,
And kings and princes, and the mighty, foil—
His ways are marvellous and manifold;
He taketh 'way the knowledge of the old.
The mighty from his power is not exempt;
He looketh on the princes with contempt.
Profound and hidden things doth he reveal,
And nothing from him doth the dark conceal.
Thro' him the nations do themselves maintain;
Should he destroy, he doth enlarge again.
He leadeth people of th' earth astray—
They grope in darkness, and they lose their way.
All this mine eye hath seen, that it is good;
All this mine ear hath heard and understood.

For what ye know I also know the same,
And equal judgment with you do I claim.
I would of th' Almighty now enquire;
To speak and reason with him I desire.
For ye, I do not trust—to me ye lie,
No comfort doth your partial words supply.
Oh that ye would forever hold your peace—
At least, until your wisdom shall increase.
For reasoning old age should man equip;
Now hearken to the pleadings of my lip.
Will ye, for God, speak wickedly and dim?
And will ye talk deceitfully for him?
Shall I believe it true that God did send,
As deputies, *ye*, with me to contend?
Or do ye stand in mocking attitude?
If so, he surely will rebuke thy mood.
Are not ye of his mightiness afraid?
And do ye not his wrath and vengence dread?
Let me alone, and hold your peace—be still
That I may speak—let come to me what will.
My confidence in God has burst afresh;
To him I now commit both soul and flesh.
Although he slay me, yet in him I'll trust.
And my salvation with him I intrust.
Hear ye my declarations with your ears;
I shall be justified; I have no fears.
Is not there one to plead from you among?
For I shall die now, if I hold my tongue.
But only two things grant, thou God, to me,
Then call, and speak, and I will answer thee.
I beg thou wilt, from me, thy hand withdraw,
And frighten not me with thy dread and awe.

Show to me my transgression and my sin,
And when did mine iniquities begin.
But wherefore dost thou hide from me thy face,
And let thine enemy thy gifts debase?
Will thou pursue and break a driven leaf?
Thou mak'st me doubly conscious of my grief.
Thou lookest narrowly unto my ways.
Why shouldst thou with affliction fill my days?
Man born of woman 's of few days of gloom,
And trouble brings him to an early tomb.
He cometh forth as flowers of the field,
That are cut down ere they their fragrance yield.
And dost thou ope thine eyes on such an one?
My days of life have to their limit run ;
My bounds are fixed so that I cannot pass ;
Long years do restless days and nights amass.
The life of trees, tho' hewn, doth never cease,
For tender branches sprout and will increase ;
Though root, and stock thereof, die in the ground,
It will, by watering, with buds abound.
But man is weakened—dies—and where is he?
He drieth up like waters of the sea.
He riseth not till heaven is no more.
From death, wilt thou, to man new life restore?
I will abide my time and wait my change,
And for a life of joy I will arrange.
Iniquity and sin thou dost observe,
And for the sinful man thy wrath reserve.
For sin, corruption doth his life curtail,
And those against him ever do prevail.
His sons are honored, he doth not perceive,
His sons are slain—and he can only grieve.

And pain and anguish by him shall be borne,
Until his very soul in him shall mourn."

PART THE THIRD.

I.

Then Eliphaz again replied,
For Job himself had justified.
"Shall wise man utter knowledge vain? or reason
With unprofitable talk? or speak
Where he can do no good? Thou castest off
Thy fear, and thou dost choose the crafty's tongue.
Thy mouth doth utter thine iniquity.
Thy own mouth doth condemn thee, and not I.
Against thee do thine own lips testify.
Art thou the first man that was born? Or wast
Thou made before the hills? What knowest thou
That we know not? What understandest thou
That we do not? With us are aged men,
And gray-haired men much older than thy father.
Are consolations small with thee from God?
Why doth thine heart take thee away, that thou,
'Gainst God, shouldst turn thy spirit, and allow
Such words as thou hast spoken 'scape thy mouth?
And why should man be clean? And he which is
Of woman born be righteous in God's sight?
Behold, no trust he putteth in his saints,
And in his sight, the heavens are not clean.
And how much more abom'nable is man.
Now hear me and I will declare to thee
What men of wisdom from their fathers told;
They unto whom, alone, th' earth was given.
The wicked man travaileth all his days

With pain—is in prosperity destroyed;
And for his bread he wandereth abroad.
Against him grief and anguish shall prevail,
Because he stretcheth out his hand 'gainst God.
He dwelleth in cities desolate and ruin'd;
And he shall not be rich, nor shall his wealth
Continue; he shall not depart from darkness.
Let the deceiv'd trust not in vanity,
For vanity shall be his recompense.
The congregation of the hypocrite
Shall perish, for they bring forth vanity;
And mischief and deceit do they conceive."

Then Job made answer to his friends.
" No sympathy your words attends;
Poor sympathizers are ye all.
Why didst thou answer?   Did I call?
If my soul were in your souls stead,
Then I could at you shake my head.
But I would seek to give relief
By words that would assuage your grief.
Although I speak my grief is there;
I am not eased tho' I forbear.
But now ye all have tortured me,
Made desolate my company.
With wrinkles ye have filled my brow;
In mis'ry I before you bow.
My friends, ye with unkindness speak;
Reproachfully, ye smite my cheek.
God hath my supplication spurn'd,
And hath me to the wicked turn'd.

JOB.

He closed mine eyes, as in the dark,
And set me up to be his mark.
His archers compass me around,
And bring me bleeding to the ground.
My suff'ring bids these tears to rise ;
The shade of death is on mine eyes.
'Tis thro' injustice I endure
My grief ; my life and prayer are pure—
So cover not O Earth my blood ;
Let be as proof, this gory flood.
Behold, my record is on high ;
My witness is 'fore heaven's eye.
My friends did scorn and at me swore—
But tears to God mine eyes outpour.
Oh that a man, with God, might plead
For man ; but 'tis not so decreed.
A few years will life's taper burn,
Then I shall go to ne'er return.
A few more years of grief to brave,
Then I am ready for the grave.
With me Oh God are they that mock ;
Mine enemies around me flock.
Oh God thy shelter I request ;
Then who is he that will contest ?
For knowledge from them thou hast hid,
And exaltation hast forbid.
They who, with flatt'ry, friends assail,
Their children's eyes shall even fail.
Affliction hath bedimmed mine eye ;
The fountain of my thoughts is dry.
This shall the upright man outwit,
And stir him 'gainst the hypocrite.

The righteous shall hold on his way,
The clean shall stronger grow each day.
But as for you, I bid ye go,
For me no wisdom can ye show.
My days of purposes are past,
And heart and hope are fading fast.
The day is changing into night,
And darkness supersedes the light.
And now the grave I will await;
Till then my grief will not abate.
All yearning for this life has fled,
And hope which filled my heart is dead."

II.

Then Bildad spake to Job again,
And urged him patience to maintain.
" When will ye make an end of such words? Mark,
And afterwards then we will speak. As beasts,
Why are we in your sight reputed vile?
Shall every one forsake the earth for thee?
The wicked's spark of life shall be put out,
And darkness shall be in his house. His light
Shall be put out with him. His strength shall fail.
He walketh into nets and 'pon a snare;
The robber 'gainst him ever shall prevail;
Destruction shall await on every side,
And shall consume his strength. His confidence
Shall flee, and bring him to the king of terrors.
Then brimstone shall be scattered on his house;
His memory shall perish from th' earth,
And in the street no one shall call his name.

JOB.

He shall be driven into darkness. He
Shall son nor nephew have, nor shall
There anyone remain within his house.
They that come after him shall be surprised,
As he affrighted those that lived with him.
Such is the fate of him that knows not God."

Then Job to him this answer made:
"When will ye cease to me upbraid?
When will ye cease to vex my soul?
Can not your mouth your words control?
Ye have me these ten times reproach'd;
Ye have with cruelty approach'd.
And if it be that I have err'd,
My error is within interr'd.
If 'gainst me ye will make your plea,
Then know, God hath encompassed me.
Behold, in vain I cry aloud;
No judgment is to me allow'd.
He kills my hope on every side,
His love with me doth not abide.
Against me he hath stirred his wrath;
His troops encamp around my path;
He hath my brethren from me led;
My friends of former days have fled;
My maids e'en at me take affright;
I am alien in their sight.
My wife doth not me recognize;
My children look and then despise;
My inward friends behold with terror;
My loved ones turn from me with horror.

Have pity on me oh my friend!
Wilt thou no pitying hand extend?
Why dost thou still me persecute?
Why wilt thou leave me destitute?
Oh that my words were now preserv'd,
Or in a rock were deeply carv'd.
I know that my redeemer lives,
And he to me salvation gives.
Tho' worms this body shall destroy,
With God shall be my birth of joy.
Then I, myself, shall him behold,
And share his blessings manifold."

III.

Then Zophar spake to Job again,
The wicked's portion to explain.
"My thoughts cause me to hasten a reply,
For I have heard the check of my reproach.
Dost thou not know, since man was placed on earth,
That joy and triumph of the hypocrite
And wicked are but for a moment? He
Shall perish, and be fleeting as a dream.
Yea, he shall fade as visions of the night.
The poor shall then oppress his children, and
Tho' wickedness be sweet to him, and though
He clings to it, and doth not it forsake,
Yet, it shall be as gall of asps in him.
He shall not see the rivers or the brooks.
That which he labored for he shall restore,
Because he hath oppressed the poor, and too,
Because he took away to not regive.

JOB.

He shall not save of that which he desired,
And in prosperity shall be in straits.
Upon him shall the hand of trouble come;
Against him God shall cast his wrath.   Th' earth
Shall rise against him; his iniquity
The heavens shall reveal; his increase shall
Depart.   His goods shall flow away.   This is
The portion of the wicked man from God."

Job answered then and said, "I seek
Your privilege to let me speak.
With diligence now hear my speech;
I will ye sense and wisdom teach.
Did I, to *man*, make my complaint?
Did I, you, of my grief acquaint?
Look unto me and be surprised;
Let not your wonder be disguised.
Why do the wicked live and thrive?
The righteous with affliction strive?
The sinful man is safe from fear;
No grief or trouble cometh near;
He spends his days in joy and mirth;
But then—the grave receives from earth.
To God, therefore, a cry they raise—
'We ask no knowledge of thy ways—
Why should we homage to thee pay?
Or why should we unto thee pray?'
No good doth from their hand proceed,
Their counsel doth the good impede.
But oft destruction is their end,
For God they can not long offend.

They of God's wrath and rage shall drink,
And from his mighty anger shrink.
The happy and unhappy die,
And food for worms alike supply.
I see your cunning—know your thought,
And am aware of what ye sought.
Know ye, destruction is reserv'd
For men of sin—by them deserv'd.
Who shall to him his way declare?
The hand of death God will not spare.
How then ye comfort me in vain,
When in your answers lies remain?"

JOB.

PART THE FOURTH.

I.

Then Eliphaz an answer made,
And spake again to Job, and said:
"Can man be profitable unto God?
If so, does his success depend thereon?
Doth God take pleasure in thy righteousness?
And art thy perfect ways a gain to him?
Thy wickedness and thine iniquities
Are great. The naked thou hast stripped of clothing;
Thou hast not given water to the weary;
And from the hungry thou withheld thy bread.
About thee, therefore, snares are set; and fear
And darkness come upon and trouble thee.
In heaven there is God. Behold the stars
How high they are! Thou sayest then of God,
'What knoweth he? Can he judge thro' the clouds?'
Remembr'st thou the way which wicked men
Have trod of old—they which bade God depart?
They were cut down, and out of time destroy'd.
Acquaint thyself with God and be at peace.
Then good shall come to thee. Receive, I pray,
His law; lay up his words within thy heart.
If thou returnest to th' Almighty, thou
Shalt be built up, and thou shalt lay up gold
As stones; and thy defence shall be in him.
For then shalt thou have thy delight in God,
And unto him shalt lift thy face in prayer,
And he shall hear and harken unto thee."

Job said, "Your words create despair.
My grief is more than I can bear.
Oh that I knew where God to find,
To have my guilt and sin defin'd.
I would to him commit my case,
And argue with him face to face.
His words of answer I would know;
Thro' him I would in wisdom grow.
He would not 'gainst me raise his voice,
But in new strength would I rejoice.
His being doth mine eyes deceive;
His presence I cannot perceive;
Yet he doth see and know my way—
To him the darkness is as day.
In *his* paths I have always stepp'd,
And his commandments I have kept.
I ever have esteemed his word;
With reverence have his counsel heard.
But God's decree's immutable,
His law and mind unchangeable.
Appointed things he doth perform,
And man must to his law conform.
His presence, therefore, troubles me,
His presence which I cannot see.
Why does a man in sin persist?
Why should a man God's love resist?
God's love exceeds his law, he knows,
And oft man's sin unpunished goes.
The wicked then the poor oppress,
They bring to want the fatherless.
They sow their crime in fertile fields;
Abundant then their harvest yields.

They strew th' earth with crimes untold;
The naked leave to winter's cold,
And take the substance of the poor—
Yet fearless walks the evil-doer.
The wicked oft 'gainst God rebel,
And still in peace and quiet dwell.
The wounded men and women groan,
God hears, but answers not, their moan.
Yet God the wicked's way observes,
And for them judgment he reserves.
They are exalted, then brought low,
By God—they must reap what they sow.
My brethren will ye say I lie?
To prove me wrong I ye defy."

II.

Again to Job then Bildad spake,
And briefly did his answer make.
"Fear and dominion are with God, and peace
He maketh. Is there any number of
His troops? 'Pon whom doth not his light arise?
How then can man be justified with God?
The moon and stars in his sight are not pure;
Then how much less is man, that is a worm?"

Then Job made answer to them all,
And to them said: "Your words appall.
Didst thou ere shield the weak from harm?
Or strengthen thou the weakened arm?
Or counselled him who's weak in mind?
To suff'ring poor hast thou been kind?

To whom hast thou spoke words of cheer?
Thy words to me are not sincere.
God sees the bottom pits of hell;
His eyes on all creation dwell;
He stretcheth north o'er empty place;
He hangs the earth in lucid space;
He binds the waters in the clouds;
They hang o'er earth like fun'ral shrouds.
He holds the waters in their bounds;
And man and beast alike confounds,
The heavens tremble at his word;
By him the roaring sea is heard;
Its billows at his voice are still;
The proud yield to his mighty will.
Men fear and quake at his command.
Who can his power understand?
As God lives who hath my soul vex'd,
And with his judgment me perplex'd,
My tongue shall utter no deceit;
In all things I will be discreet.
Thou, God, I will not justify;
I will be upright till I die.
My righteousness I will hold fast,
And keep my heart clean to the last.
Doth hope, the hypocrite console
When God hath taken 'way his soul?
Will God list to the wicked's wail
When trouble 'gainst them doth prevail?
The works of God I will reveal
To you; his law I'll not conceal.
The portion of the wicked man,
Alloted by God's wond'rous plan,

JOB.

Is this : his children shall be spread
O'er earth, and they shall long for bread.
And they that with him still abide,
Grief, sorrow, death shall them betide.
Though they shall gold and silver hoard,
No blessings will their wealth afford.
Great fears shall fill their souls with dread
And terrors shall make them afraid.
For God shall not the wicked spare,
But judgment for them will prepare.
For gold and silver there's a vein ;
From earth we iron do obtain ;
To sable night there is an end ;
Earth's revolutions floods attend ;
Its bowels yield gold and sapphire ;
And from it leaps the liquid fire
With heated boulders,—moulten rocks—
Its rumbling hill and mountain shocks.
But these are only natural things—
A sense which finite knowledge brings.
But where can wisdom—mind—be found ?
Not in the sky or sea or ground.
The depth saith : 'It is not in me.'
The sea saith : 'It is not in me.'
Man knoweth not its wond'rous price ;
For barter, gold can not suffice :
Nor can this treasure silver buy ;
'Tis brilliant as the starry sky.
A matchless gem—its price untold ;
Above the ruby, crystal, gold ;
The topaz cannot equal it—
Nor diamonds brighter rays emit.

From whence—what place—doth wisdom come?
This strength to which all beasts succumb?
'Tis hidden from all living eyes,
And man doth not its power prize,
God doth this veil of mystery lift;
It is to man—from him—a gift.
A gift divine—unbounded—deep;
A gift to man—alone—to keep.
Men's sceptre as thro' life they plod,
For wisdom is a gift from God.

Oh! for the vanished past, those days
Of honor, fortune, wealth and praise;
When God from out the heavens above,
Looked down on me with boundless love.
The nobles then would give me ear,
And kings and princes did me fear.
I hearkened to the needy's voice,
And made the widow's heart rejoice.
I was a father to the poor;
A foe unto the evil-doer.
Men waited, and my counsel heard,
And then kept silence at my word.
Grave men would listen to my speech;
I would the wise and learned teach.
To me men did their trials bring;
I sat as chief and dwelt as king.
I thought my days would multiply,
Then to my home return and die.
But now the young men me deride;
Young men whose fathers I defied;

And whom I treated with disdain—
Nor dogs their fellowship would deign.
From want and famine, they, alone,
Fled to the woods with grief and groan.
Base knaves they were, and fools by birth,
Yea, they were viler than th' earth.
Their children now against me war;
They spare me not and me abhor.
Upon my right arise the youth,
With accusations of untruth.
With wickedness they mar my path;
They further my distress by wrath.
Their terrors are upon me turn'd;
My soul they curs'd—my pleadings spurn'd.
And now my trust,—my hope—is kill'd;
My days are with affliction fill'd;
Oh God! I lift my voice on high,
But thou dost not regard my cry.
Thou hast opposed me with thy hand;
The wicked mock by thy command.
I know thou wilt recall thy breath;
I know thou wilt bring me to death.
Did I not for the troubled weep?
The poor from want and famine keep?
When good I sought, then evil came;
When light I sought, then darkness came.

God doth a punishment decree
For workers of iniquity.
Doth he not see my steps and ways?
My mode of life his law obeys.

If I have failed to walk aright,
Or to be righteous in God's sight.
Let me be weighed in balance, so
That God my honesty may know.
If sin my feet has e'er beguil'd,
Or wickedness my heart defil'd,
Then let me sow and others eat,
And me of all my substance cheat.
If women have deceived my heart,
Then let my wife from me depart.
For this is a most hienous crime,
The vilest, basest sin of time.
If I despise my servants' cause,
Shall I contend with God's own laws?
For he, alike hath fashioned us,
And gave us being marvellous.
If I withheld the poor's desire,
Or 'gainst the widow did conspire,
If I have seen the naked perish,
Or from my door the needy banish,
If I abused the fatherless,
Or did not help those in distress,
Then let my arm be broke in twain,
Let God his anger not restrain.
I am not from God's wrath secure,
His power I could not endure.
If gold has been my confidence,
Or hoarded wealth with love intense,
(For this is to a sin allied,
As I should then have God denied)
If my heart did with joy abound,
When evil my oppressors found,

Or to their souls did wish a curse,
Then prove me sinful and perverse.
Oh would that God would answer me,
My righteousness and virtue see."

Then Job no more spake to his friends,
And with these words his answer ends.

PART THE FIFTH.

I.

So these men ceased to Job advise,
As he was righteous in his eyes.
Then Elihu, son of Barachel,
Was wroth with Job, his friends as well.
At Job, for he had justified
Himself, and, therefore, God defied.
His friends, for they could not contend
With Job, and yet did him condemn.
Elihu waited till Job spake,
Before he did his answer make.
"Now I am young and ye are very old;
I feared, therefore, to show you mine opinion.
I said that many years should wisdom teach.
But great men are not always wise, nor do
The aged judgment understand. I said,
I, therefore, mine opinion, too, will show.
I waited for your words and unto them
Gave ear, and there was none that answered Job.
Ye were amazed—ye answered not his words.
When I had waited (for they spake no more)
I said, I, too, will mine opinion show.
For I am full of words, and I will speak
That I may be refreshed. I pray thee Job,
My speeches hear, and hearken to my words.
My lips shall utter knowledge clearly, and
My words shall be of purity of heart.

If thou canst answer, stand and give thy words.
Behold, I am, according to thy wish,
In God's stead.   I am also formed of clay.
Now thou hast spoken, and I heard thee say
That thou wert clean without transgressions, thou
Wert innocent, with no iniqity,
And God had marked thy path.   Behold, I say,
In this thou art not just, for God is greater
Than man.   Then why dost thou against him strive?
For of his ways he giveth not account.
He calleth man in visions to repent,
And by afflictions, and his ministry.
God taketh 'way his meat ; his life he giveth
Unto destroyers—his soul unto the grave.
If there be an interpreter to show
To man his uprightness ; then he to man
Is gracious, for he found a ransom.   Then
He unto God shall pray and see his face.
Lo, all these things God worketh oftentimes
With man, to flood his soul with living light.
Mark well O Job and hearken unto me,
And hold thy peace ; I shall thee wisdom teach.

Ye wise men, hear my words ! and give me ear
Ye men of knowledge !   Let us judgment choose ;
For Job hath said that he is righteous, and
That God hath taken 'way his judgment, and
It profits naught to delight himself with God.
Ye wise men, therefore, hearken unto me !
God *will not* do or work iniquity,
And *can* not be unjust.   The works of men
He unto them shall render.   Who, o'er earth,

Hath given him a charge—the world dispos'd?
If he should set his heart 'pon man, all flesh
Shall perish—man be turned again to dust.
Should subjects charge a king with wickedness?
Then how much less him that regardeth not
The rich more than the poor? They are his works.
He seeth all the acts and deeds of man—
The wicked can not hide themselves from him—
He striketh mighty men as wicked men,
Because they would consider not his ways.
Who can make trouble when he peace doth give,
Whether 'gainst a nation or a man?
'Tis meet for man to say to God that he
Hath borne chastisement and will sin no more.
Now Job hath spoken words devoid of wisdom.
Because of such words let him then be tried,
For he doth add rebellion unto sin.
Didst thou think it was right to speak of God
And say thy righteousness wert more than his?
Thou saidst: 'What profit it if I be cleans'd?'
Look at the heavens and behold the clouds—
If thou shouldst sin, what doest thou to him?
If thou be righteous, what doth he receive?
By reason of the mighty, th' oppress'd
Cry out, but are not heard for want of faith.
For vanity God will not hear. He hath,
In anger, visited, yet Job knew not.
So, therefore, Job doth ope his mouth in vain.
Now bear with me awhile—I will show thee
That I have yet to speak on God's behalf.
God is in strength and wisdom mighty, and
Despiseth none; doth spare the wicked's life;

Nor from the righteous doth withdraw his eyes,
And kings doth he establish on their thrones,
If they obey him, in prosperity
They spend their days; in pleasure spend their years.
E'en so would he afflicton have removed
From thee, but thou fulfilled the wicked's judgment.
Will he esteem thy riches? no, nor gold.
Take heed—regard thou not iniquity.
Remember that thou magnify his work,
Which men behold, that every man may see.
Behold—God is great—we know him not.
He maketh small the drops of water, till,
According to the vapor, down they pour.
Can any understand the sun, the clouds?
But he, by them, the needs of men doth judge.
At this my heart doth tremble and is mov'd
Out of its place.   Attentively hear God.
His voice doth thunder marv'lously; great things
He doeth which we cannot comprehend.
He saith unto the snow: 'Be thou on earth;'
He sealeth up the hand of every man;
He maketh beasts go into dens; from north
He sendeth cold—the whirlwind from the south.
The frost is given by the breath of him.
Now hearken unto this O Job; stand still.
Consider, thou, the wond'rous works of God.
Dost thou know when he caused the light to shine?
Or dost thou know the balancings of clouds?
Dost thou know why the winds from south are warm?
Didst thou with him spread out the glitt'ring sky?
Then teach us what we shall say unto him.
Shall it be told him that I speak?   If man

Shall speak he surely shall be swallowed up.
Men do not see the bright light thro' the clouds.
In power, justice he is excellent;
And he is terrible in majesty.
Men, therefore, fear him. He will not afflict,
But he doth not respect the wise of heart."

JOB.

PART THE SIXTH.

I.

The Lord, himself, to Job then spake,
And did an answ'ring challenge make.
"Who is this that counsel darkeneth
By words devoid of knowledge? Gird thy loins
Now, like a man, for answer I'll demand.
Where wast thou when I set the bounds of earth?
If thou hast understanding, then declare.
Now whereupon are the foundations fastened?
Who laid the corner stone thereof—the day
When all the sons of God did shout for joy,
And when the morning stars together sang?
Or who shut up the sea with bars and doors,
And bade it hither, but no further, come?
Hast thou commanded morning since thy days,
That it might shake the wicked out of earth?
Light is withholden from the wicked man.
Hast thou walked into the sea, or search'd its depths?
Or have the gates of death been oped to thee?
Hast thou perceived the length and breadth of earth?
If thou dost know it all, declare. Dost thou
Know where the darkness and the light doth dwell?
Wast thou born then? Art thou so great in years?
Hast thou e'er seen the treasures of the snow?
Or hast thou seen the treasures of the hail,
Which I've reserved against the time of war?
Who hath a way divided for the thunder,
To cause it on the wilderness to rain,
To make the tender herbs to shoot and bud?

Hath rain a father, and the drops of dew?
Or canst thou loose Orion's band, or bind
The sweet influences of Pleiades?
In season canst thou bring forth Mazzaroth?
Or canst thou guide Acturus, with his sons?
Dost thou the ordinances of heaven know?
Canst thou from clouds send thunder, lightnings, rain?
And who hath given knowledge to the heart?
Or who provideth for the raven food?
Dost thou know who hath set the wild ass free?
He doth the multitude of cities scorn,
And roams the wilderness and barren land.
Or canst thou trust and bind th' unicorn?
Didst thou give to the peacocks goodly wings?
Or didst thou give the horse his strength and cloth'd
His neck with thunder? Canst thou make him fear?
He paweth and rejoiceth in his strength;
At fear he mocketh and is not afraid.
At thy command doth th' eagle soar above
And make her nest on high among the rocks,
From whence she, for her young, doth seek the prey?
Shall he that doth contend with God instruct him?
He that reproveth God, shall answer it."

Then Job answered the Lord and said:
"Behold, I'm vile—what shall I answer thee?
I'll lay my hand upon my mouth. I've spoken
Once—yea twice; but will proceed no further."

The Lord then answered Job and said:
"Gird up thy loins, now like a man. I will
Demand of thee; declare thou unto me.

Wilt thou my judgment also disannul,
And me condemn, that thou may'st righteous be?
Hast thou an arm like God? or voice like him?
Now deck thyself with majesty; thyself
Array with beauty; cast abroad thy wrath,
And every one that's proud, seek and abase,
And bring him low; and tread the wicked down;
Then unto thee I also will confess
That thine own hand can save thee. Now, behold
Behemoth; he doth eat grass as an ox;
His strength is in his loins; his bones are strong
As bars of iron, or as bars of brass.
He is the chief of all the beasts of God.
He lieth under shady trees in fens;
Will any take him in his sight?
Canst thou draw out Leviathan with a hook?
Will he make supplication unto thee?
Wilt thou with him play as with birds? Or shall
They part him 'mong the merchants? Lay thine hand
Upon him, then remember—do no more.
The hope of him is vain; at sight of him
Is one cast down; none is so fierce that dare
To stir him up. Who then can stand 'fore me?
For all that under heaven is, is mine."

II.

Then Job submitted to God's word,
And answ'ring said unto the Lord:
"I know thou canst do everything;
And canst man to submission bring.
No thought can be withheld from thee,
No deed be done thou canst not see.

I've uttered that I fathomed not—
Things wonderful which *I* knew not.

So now, my words I beg thee hear—
Give to my supplications ear.
Before, of thee I only *heard*,
I *see* thee now and hear thy word.
I, therefore, all my ways lament,
And in the dust I now repent."

III.

When Job had this confession made,
The Lord to Eliphaz then said:
"'Gainst thee and thy two friends my wrath is kindl'd,
For ye have spoken not of me the thing
That's right, as hath my servant Job. So now
Take seven rams and seven bullocks to
My servant Job, and offer up yourselves
Burnt offerings; and Job shall pray for you—
For him will I accept; unless I deal
With you according to your folly, for
Ye have not spoken of me right, as Job."

IV.

They could no longer Job withstand,
And did as God did them command.
Then God to Job did joy restore,
And doubled what he had before.
The Lord thus blessed his latter end,
And wealth and happiness did send.
For seven score years Job did abide
On earth; then being old he died.

ON MY TWENTY-FIFTH BIRTHDAY.

(April 8th, 1897, 12 Midnight.)

One quarter in the century's past,
   And I am still alive ;
Another toll recalls the fact
   That I am twenty-five.

With humble thanks to crown the fact
   That I am still alive ;
Distressing thought succeeds the fact
   That I am twenty-five.

The past reviewed is endless waste ;
   An ocean's depth to dive—
A feat I don't propose to try
   At age of twenty-five.

The now engages present thought,
   Of how with time to strive ;
The future bursts with sudden glare
   At end of twenty-five.

Encumbered with an earthly state,
   I manage to derive,
A much diluted blessing from
   The age of twenty-five.

Assurance of a *worse* estate,
   Constrains me to contrive,
To feel I'm blessed (in masquerade)
   This year of twenty-five.

ON MY TWENTY-FIFTH BIRTHDAY.

For patronage, by duty forced,
   I'm called upon to drive
In double-harnessed gratitude
   O'er all those twenty-five.

To toss in quite a shipwrecked style,
   Tends only to deprive
One of the chance to see he's blessed,
   At drifting twenty-five.

A generous public—liberal world—(?)
   With ignorance doth connive,
To don a palsied, envious air,
   Round me at twenty-five.

The world exclaims: "You're truly blessed,"
   The kinship hoax revive—
With interest-bearing kinship bonds
   At age of twenty-five.

The active bees hum thro' the world,
   And stock their little hive—
With single thought, insanely weak—
   I've found at twenty-five.

I've got a roof above my head;
   (My obligations thrive)
One suit of clothes, one hat and a dog,
   At age of twenty-five.

I've got my health—that blessing sure—
   And struggle to derive
Some comfort from two meals a day,
   At age of twenty-five.

THE BELLS.

I've credit also (blessing 2)
   Serene demands arrive—
And blessings swell while pockets shrink ;
   At blessed twenty-five.

Misfortune swings a flaming torch—
   Its heat I *can* survive ;
Again a blessing—*unconsumed*
   Clear up to twenty-five.

I've safely sailed the boisterous course,
   And I am yet alive—
With humble hopes of weathering through
   Another twenty-five.

THE BELLS.

(With apologies to Edgar A. Poe.)

Hear the nation with the Bells,—
   Bryan bells !
What a tale of happiness their melody foretells.
   How they tinkle, tinkle, tinkle,
     Thro' the land from morn till night !
   While the opposition's jeering,
   All the people still are cheering
     With a genuine delight;
    Keeping time, time, time,
     With the harmony of rhyme,

To the rapture of the prophesy that confidently wells
    From the bells, bells, bells,
        Bells, bells, bells, bells—
To the Bryan and the Sewall of the bells!

Hear the Democratic bells—
    Silver bells!
What a reign of peacefulness their harmony foretells.
    In the sequel to the race,
    What a promise they embrace!
    As the mellow music floats,
        And all in tune,
    What a myriad of votes,
With significance will rally to the notes,
        Very soon!
Oh, throughout this glorious land,
Listen to the music of the silver laden band,
      How it swells!
      How it dwells
    On the future! How it tells
    Of the shadow it dispels
By the swinging and the ringing of the William Bryan bells.
    Of the bells, bells, bells,
      Bells, bells, bells, bells—
By the chiming of the Bryan-Sewall bells.

Hear the opposition bells—
    Golden bells!
What a train of gloomy fears their jarring tone compels.
    What a dreary dirge they toll!
    How their dismal echoes roll!

THE BELLS. 51

    For encouragement they seek ;
    Only hear them shriek, shriek, shriek,
       In despair !
In a powerless appealing, with the knowledge of defeat,
With the knowledge, forced upon them, of a very bad defeat,
    Sinking lower, lower, lower,
    Conscious they can never more—
    Unavailing to endeavor—
    Hope to occupy—ah never—
Occupy the presidential chair.
    Oh, the bells, bells, bells!
    How their feeble tone foretells
      Hope forlorn !
   How they sob and sigh and moan ;
     What an agonizing groan
Is predicted for the near election morn!
   Oh, the Goldbug fully knows
    By the twanging,
    And the clanging,
How the pop'lar current flows.
    And the sound distinctly tells,
     In the chiming,
     And the rhyming,
   How enthusiasm swells
By the ringing and the jingling of the Bryan-Sewall bells!
    Of the bells, bells, bells,
By the rhyming and the chiming of the bells.

[Published in the "Public Ledger," Norfolk, Va., Sept. 11,'96.]

TO MY FATHER.

On the Birth of my Brother, the Last.

Another babe! another boy!
A fleeting product—transient joy!
A bubble blown by '94,
With all its mis'ries (may be more;)
Born ere the Old Year's dying sigh
Proclaimed its death—its passage by
The halls of time, into the past;
The month, the twelfth; the day, the last.
Of offsprings, last. So was he born,
At December's chilly break of morn.

Ye Gods! how nature did encase,
Her bounty to eternize the race,
Within a zealous keeper's frame;
A herd perpetuate his name.

And canst thou give a reason why
That mournful man is born to die?
Bend low thine ear the cradle o'er,
And catch the answer, baby lore,
Fresh from th' eternal realms above,
With perfumed breath of angels' love—
And ask that little babe, I say,
Whence comes this sorrow-laden day;
This life—*one day*—'tis all we get;
Each moment's joy breeds but regret.

TO MY FATHER.

Methinks an inward echo'd speak:
"God said he would his vengeance wreak
On fallen man; and so his doom,
Shall ever be an early tomb."
Yet speechless is that little tongue;
What truths are there, are left unsung.
No hidden secret 'scapes his breast—
A mine of wealth, with means unblest
To gather from the treasure-cave;
Not e'en the power those gems to save.
Ah yes! he knows, but coming years
Exchange the purities for fears.
Then chaos chains the infant mind,
And leaves the *brightest* thoughts behind.

And by my faith! excuse this burst
Of—nothing. (Of the two, the worst.)
But to resume my former speech:
(I'll stick to this, now, like a leech,)
I was a-speaking of the bliss,
Concomitant to gifts like this.
A New Year's gift it might have been;
A precious gift—a "child of sin."

But not to lose the story's thread—
Do not you more the future dread,
With all those little mouths to feed,
Those backs to clothe? Apply the reed—
(You call to mind that counsel mild,
To "spare the rod and spoil the child").
Take heed,—and ere his errant ways,
Embitter your declining days—

TO MY FATHER.

Direct and guide him in the path
Of right,—but hold within your *wrath*.

I see I'm running off again ;
You'll pardon this suggestive vein.
I meant to talk with lighter heart,
But still, it seems, I will depart
From wholesome mirth, that joyous chime,
To labor through some weighty rhyme.

The baby's born! he's come to stay!
He'll be man, I hope and pray ;
A grocery man, with stately mein,
A-testing Oleo-Margarine.
To herrings may his fancy take,
Or in the oven biscuits bake.
Or still there's lard and coffee, too,
Or meat to run the trier through.
Or butter— oh! that's cousin Ben's—
Or catching skippers thro' the lens.
Excuse me if I add to these,
Digesting strong and aged cheese.
All this time will occupy
Through life—his head get bald—then die.

A happy man he'd prove to be,
Could he but through the future see.
A lucky chap—most lucky one,
By being born the *youngest* son.
To him a father leaves his wealth
(Purchased by his broken health,)

TO MY FATHER.

His life will be serene and calm,
A-sampling flour, smelling ham ;
In tricks of trade he'll be instilled;
With knowledge "cured" his head be filled ;
With "sugared" words his speech will flow,
As oft he finds the market low.
And "canvassed" goblins rob his sleep ;
And oft a "briny" tear he'll weep.
Then "pickled" malice strong and loud,
His finer feelings sadly cloud.
"Ah me ! and this" (it will be said)
Is why poor Mr. D. is dead."

Again my pen has lost its way ;
Perchance you'll think it doth inveigh
Against this little "kooing kid";
(With no intention, if it did.)
A name ! A name ! I want a name !
A sound to set the world aflame ;
An appellation fit to be
A handle to the surname D.
This is the hour's crying need,
For (like the 'possum) we are treed."
Cognomens we can not supply;
What *shall* we call this little fry ?
There's Harry, Clara, Will and Nan,
(That number's 'nough for any man)
By Jove ! but that is only half—
(This matter doth evoke a laugh)
Then Marvin, Alice and—Lamar—
(The noblest and the best by far.)
Now isn't that a goodly pack ?
No wonder then a name we lack.

TO MY FATHER.

You'll pardon my advising mood—
(From such much good has ne'er accrued—)
Prefix a name of any sort,
But *don't* you call him Jim, " for short."
While speaking through such rambling verse,
'Tis forethought to be short and terse.
But while 'tis true I ought to quit,
I'll have one more euphonious fit.

Convey my blessings to the boy;
May happiness, without alloy,
Contribute to his stock of life,
To sweeten some the bitter strife.
He's welcome to our world of groan,
Where most the songs end with a moan.
Come little one, give us thy hand,
We'll lead you through this cursed land,
Where every demon grins to see
His brother in adversity.
Sweet innocence, thy little brain,
Knows not the agonizing pain
That permeates this sinful world,
From battlements of heaven hurl'd.

We still, this little stranger greet;
To humble fare, we will him treat;
And should his days be lengthened here,
Like guardian angels, hover near.

A LETTER TO NANNIE.

How goes the world, my sister Nan,
  Within the classic boundary?
I guess they've got the furnace hot,
  In that old mental foundry.
The spirit urged me let you hear
  Of my unceased existence;
And so in lieu of worshipping,
  I offered no resistance.

For just a line, I claim conceit
  Of welcome, kind reception;
So here she goes—my bark of rhyme,
  And steered to all the deep shun.
But should these lines divorce your thoughts,
  When by the midnight taper,
Just roll them in convenient shape
  And use as curling paper.

The topics for a minute's talk,
  Are truly widely scattered;
And should I dwell upon myself,
  I'd be too highly flattered.
H. Warren has secured a cold,
  And made an anxious mother;
And Marguerite obtained its mate,
  And hence alarmed another.

The sleet, in cool supremacy,
  Reclines upon the pavement;

The cold, in frosty impudence,
  Exhibits no abatement.
The cats are frozen 'neath the house,
  And all the pumps are ditto;
The stove, in imitative freak,
  Yields frozen meals to sit to.

The syrup's lost its liquid state;
  The milk, beyond redemption;
The butter lies quite bullet-proof,
  The rolls claim no exemption.
The cook has taken to her bed,
  (At home) in frozen slumber;
The week is frozen up so tight
  The days have lost their number.

The year is older by a month,
  And little bit the wiser;
It still retains its joys and woes,
  The rich, the poor, the miser.
The giddy whirl of fashion's coach
  Speeds with the humble wagon;
The sparkle in the rich man's glass,
  Suggests the drunkard's flagon.

The churches still uphold their end,
  And fight to be the winners;
While Dr. Young is laboring hard
  Among a flock of sinners.
That noble champion of the cause—
  (For him our love will never end!)
Has honored, once again, our town—
  Your Dr. Smith, the Reverend.

A LETTER TO NANNIE.

I think the Colonel and his aid
    Are still in winter quarters,
If Ma's not lost the movements of
    Her regimental daughter.
It grieves me to inscribe the truth,
    This fact proceeds from hearsay;
But then I must admit the truth,
    The fault's with me I dare say.

And Harry struggles with his tasks,
    Achieving monthly glory;
While conning books, is eating lead—
    (The nature of his story)
He says he's had a "chill or two"—
    "A little fever's" grieved him;
The bread is still served petrified;
    The butter's twice deceived him.

But, dearest Nan, we all are well;
    (Save two, upon reflection.)
I trust you can your picture paint
    In similar complexion.
So now, good-night—I hasten through;
    My pleasant duty's ended,
And file excuse for tiring you,
    Much more than I intended.

THE BARON AND HIS TYPEWRITIST.

(With apologies to John G. Whittier.)

Maud Fuller on a summer's day,
In seemingly a dreamy way,

Applied her fingers to the keys,
And sighed (it may be for a breeze).

The rev'rie that enthralled her soul,
Was soon beyond her sweet control;

And she was quite content to wear,
A listless mood and pensive air;

With, still the moments to beguile,
A sad and half-decided smile.

The aged pile across the street,
In fancy, seemed her mood to greet.

Its grated windows partly closed,
As if a dream within reposed.

Her drooping lids she slightly raised,
And gently, in abstraction, gazed.

The monument of ancient art
Resighed the echo of her heart.

In building same, but mood reversed,
His Nibs, the Baron, sat immersed.

The man complete, without a care,
The product of good health and fare,

Came lightly tripping o'er the floor,
And gently opened Maudie's door.

The errant gaze was quick reclaimed;
A blush bespoke her half ashamed.

The Baron, with admiring air,
Surveyed the features, dress and hair.

From shapely foot to raven crown,
His cautious eyes stole up and down.

The silent trip was hardly spent,
When Maud betrayed embarrassment.

With effort, Nibs controlled a glance—
A duplicate—and spoke by chance.

To humbly by her side to rest,
And watch her write—his sole request.

The maiden hastened to obey,
And, blushing, gave her fingers play.

Full o'er the keys the chase began,
While fancies in confusion ran.

An "L" was tapped—an instant staid
The fairy touch; a leap was made

To gently linger on an "O;"
Then onward sped the rippling flow.

Sweet visions of enchanted lands,
Obeyed the music of her hands.

A "V" was caught betwixt the spell,
And joyfully a victim fell.

(The iv'ry purely showed delight
To bear such unaccustomed fright.)

The old machine, with beaming face,
Now mustered its departing grace;

And throbbed with every fresh surprise,
As o'er it swept the hazel eyes.

Across the fields, with verdure green,
Still ever flashed the changing scene.

Adown the valley of the souls,
A melancholy cadence rolls;

Then upwards floats, with mystic rhyme,
To mingle with a sabbath chime.

Alas! the vision quickly sped,
And maid and Nibs to earth were led.

An "E" contrived to notice gain,
And so relieved the fearful strain.

The maid assumed a weary mein,
And ditto did the old machine.

The Baron from his trance awoke,
And falt'ring, thus with feeling spoke:

"A sweeter strain I never heard,
So like unto—a humming-bird;"

Proceeding wisely to dilate
Upon the weather's present state.

When scarce of reasons to remain,
Composure failing to regain,

THE BARON AND HIS TYPEWRITIST.

His Nibs his lonely bower sought,
To there regale himself in thought.

Maud Fuller sighed "Ah me!" and said :
"If I might fan the Baron's head ;

He'd need to fan to circulate
A patent breeze at cyclone rate."

The Baron lost in thought profound,
In silent survey, glanced around.

Encouraged thus to freely speak,
Exclaimed : "Could I but kiss that cheek."

Maud hammers still the iv'ry boards,
But cherished memories dearly hoards.

The parrot swings at even-tide ;
The cat reposes at her side.

The tea-leaves dubious fortunes tell ;
So Maud and cat and parrot dwell.

The Baron wed from finer caste,
With thoughts still wand'ring in the past,

While dreams of cheek and raven lock,
Would through his troubled slumbers flock.

Sometimes, at even, in the coals,
The picture of a face unrolls.

Alas for Nibs! Alas for maid ;
A perfect life was never made.

"Of all sad words of tongue or pen
The saddest are these : 'It might have been'."

ON THE OCCASION OF FINDING A YELLOW PUP.

Dame Fortune seeks in varied ways
    her children to endow;
And regulates by way of smiles,
    the portion to allow;
A certain smile denotes success
    to enterprises bold,
And speculations favored thus
    the seeds of promise hold.
Another kind may signify
    but just a little "raise,"
But that does intimation give
    of coming brighter days.
And thus a distribution wise,
    of Fortunes' hoarded pile,
Is managed and apportioned through
    the medium of her smile.
I met Dame Fortune on the street
    at dusk of yesterday;—
I felt she blessed me with a smile
    in passing on her way.
Her pensive brow became unknit,
    her mouth was wandering up;
In twenty minutes from that time
    I found a yellow pup!
I did indeed—a yellow pup!
    a whole, delightful pug!
My heart gushed forth with melted joy,
    in one embracing hug.

FINDING A YELLOW PUP.

I think I have a baby home—
                I've heard it mentioned sure—
I sheltered him (the pup, I mean,)
                behind the stove, secure.
They'll tell you home I've got a cat,
                which really may be so,
I've quite forgot—(she may be dead)—
                I fed the dog I know.
I have a dim remembrance of
                some chickens once I had;
I'll ask if they are still alive,
                (I trust he'll not go mad).

I shook the tree of lucky fruit,—
                a goodly shower fell;
But one lone fruit tenacious hung,
                resistance to the spell.
Repeated trials won success—
                I got it with a fight—
It bloomed into a yellow pup—
                my heart and soul's delight!
Canary-birds and mocking-birds
                and parrots red or green,
May serve to satisfaction give
                where pups are never seen;
But as for drawing joy from such,
                you'd better give it up;
The only 18-karat bliss
                is found in a yellow pup.

AN INCIDENT ON A STREET IN NORFOLK.

I journeyed through the crowded street
    Ere the retiring sun
Encircled earth in drowsy dusk—
    Its daily duty done.
Besides the ditch a creature crouched;
    And she was pale and wan.

The burden of misfortune's years
    Was resting on that form,
Whilst prayerful music strove to meet
    The fury of the storm.
Unconscious of a beggar's state,
    Her baby nestled warm.

The limits of a martyrdom
    Her life had closed upon;
Her cup received, with silent thanks,
    The transient notice won.
I glanced into the cup and saw
    A penny—and but *one*.

And diamonds paled the twilight hour;
    Resplendent luxury shone;
Can silken dress the tattered gown
    No recognition own?
Regardless riches sauntered near
    The rags upon the stone.

Oh weary arm! oh aching heart!
  Grind out thy mild appeal!
That lady if she *could* but hear,
  Would pitying heart reveal.
Oh weary arm, the city's deaf—
  Grind loud thy mild appeal!

I journeyed back; the hov'ring night
  Its vigils had begun;
Can silken dress with tranquil mind
  Disturbing knowledge shun?
I glanced into the cup and saw
  A penny—*still* but one.

ON THE NAMING OF HOTEL "EMORY."
Louisburg, N. C.

TO CLARA.

A couple regarded in enviable light,
  One morning an issue proclaimed;
A daughter was born,
On that memorable morn,
Predestined to rank with the famed.

The shadow of luck o'er her cradle was cast;
  Was fed on the broth of desire;
    Progressive ambition
    Insured her position
During pauses of journeying higher.

Infallible omens attended her course
O'er girlhood's most turbulent tide;
Considerate gales
Inflated her sails,
Till harbored and moored as a bride.

Protecting her ever, this guardian eye
Proceeds to immortalize worth;
So searching his memory
He recollects "Emory"
To ornament structural birth.

The couple referred to, a line or two back,
Have aged with the fleeting of years;
But oh what a pride
To their manner allied!
When "Emory" greeted their ears.

"LITTLE WILLIAM'S" THANKS.

(Supposing he could.)

TO N—— L——D.

Oh! Auntie dear, I got the pin,
        and such a lovely token;
I let no moments slip away
        with hearty thanks unspoken.

It was so thoughtful, thus to give
    such notice to a creature
So far away and little known ;
    that forms the sweetest feature.
To measure the esteem in which
    I hold your kind remembrance,
The trial would, to what I feel,
    bear only a resemblance.
But oh you can interpret this
    as deep appreciation,
With love returned, and pride expressed,
    from your six-day relation.

A SIMPLE PRAYER.

God of mercy, deal thou gently,
 With thy weak and errant son ;
Let thy hand in pity lead him
 To the path he had begun.

Let thy omnipresence shield him ;
 Let thy arms his refuge be ;
Suffer thy reflecting glory,
 Fill him with thy purity.

Pardon, thou, his human frailities ;
 Inward tempests lead astray ;
Let thy lustre of compassion
 Guide him on his rugged way.

Let thy halo of protection,
  Brilliant, ever hover near;
Bear, thou, with his fruitless struggles;
  Calm his agonizing fear.

Breathe the unction of thy spirit
  O'er his agitated soul;
Lull assailing evil's fury;
  Still the billows' angry roll.

Strenghten, thou, resistance's armor,
  When adversities assail;
Guard him on his narrow journey
  Through life's dimly-lighted vale.

AN OUTCRY.

Holy angels, to me speak—-
Chanting sweet thy melodies;
Breathe thy incense on my soul,—
Angry tempests 'round me roll—
And the demons gain control.
Oh! the ceaseless agonies
Ever gnawing at my heart.
Fainter grow I, fainter grow!
Holy angels, soothe my heart.

ON THE BIRTH OF MY SON.
April 14, 1897.
THE ARRIVAL'S SALUTE.

I'm king of the kingdom of woe—
    I'm here—alas! alack!
I greet you my sufferers below—
    To stay—alas! alack!

THE WORLD'S RETURN.

O king of the kingdom of woe—
    You'll find this a popular track!
Accept of your quota below—
    Here's luck to the journey—alack!

TO W.——P.——B.

My dear Mr. Bond, here's a letter for you,
    In answer to yours of the 8th,
(Arriving at last, after three months had passed
    Since mine of a previous date.)

I pardon omission in friends of my heart;
    Their errors I never discuss;
For gossip's a fiend that is best early weaned
    From the breast of a peace-loving cuss.

TO W.——P.——B.

So smother what fears in your mind may arise,
  Regarding the time that has fled
Since your last reply; for most truly have I;—
  Let anger go bury its dead.

The time that elapsed is my only regret;
  The fault of *neglect* I condone.
I shall not reprove, but I urge you improve
  In promptness—and promptness alone.

I offer this counsel—accept it or not;
  Impelled by the fact that I hold,
In such high esteem, all your letters,—I deem
  This impudence not overbold.

You humble yourself by a verdict too harsh;
  A judgment you do not deserve;
But self-imposed blame is concession of shame
  For actions that friends don't observe.

You say "you must think me a poor correspondent.'
  You are—measuring time by the roll;
If that is a sin you had better begin
  To pray for thy salvable soul.

But as I have said (and I say it again)
  You *merit* my modest reproach;
But as you guilt assume I shall *not* now presume,
  On justice, the least, to encroach.

To answer in sections, your valued reply,
  Would bore you entirely too long;
For writing in rhyme is a burdensome crime.—
  So I hasten the end of my song.

TO W.——P.——B.

I note your remarks in relation to Job ;
   Quotations defy all your rules ;
Allow me to say that the wisest men may,
   Unwittingly, plagiarize fools.

I own it confession of ignorance vast !—
   Surprise at its biblical source.—
Purloining the Bible exposes to libel
   Hereafter I'll alter my course.

I grant you relief from an idea you hold ;—
   Its origin *I* never knew,
But while unaware of its issue in prayer,
   I never have charged it to you.

The "nature of term and the nature of tone,"
   I know, should have guided me straight ;
But slang so prevails (under steam and with sails)
   I thought you unloaded such freight.

The tributes they paid to Fred Douglas were just ;
   (Tho' I of this meeting ne'er heard)
I assign him a place, irrespective of race,
   Above his coeval black herd.

You ask why we cherish the mem'ry of him ;
   Why "waste on the reprobate praise?"
We reverence *worth* in the South, West or North,
   And shafts in memoriam raise.

We slavishly bow before intellect's shrine ;
   Why question the color it wears ?
We honor ambition in every position ;
   Why decipher the motto it bears ?

TO W.——P.——B.

Pray do not adjudge me disloyal to birth;
   Nor couple with treason my name;
But truth is concealed behind honesty's shield—
   Let no one her virtue defame.

His struggle for knowledge, his ultimate gain;
   Compel me his spirit admire;
I heed not his birth, nor his mission on earth—
   And hatred with death should expire.

Consider your station as common with his,—
   And feel all his cravings of heart;
Would *you* not rebel against slavery's hell?
   Would *you* not from bondage depart?

John Brown was a "duck" of a far different brood;
   The rope that entwi'n'd his vile neck
Should e'en be befriended for having thus ended
   The life of this ethical wreck.

We hung up this brainless, seditious disturber—
   A just recompense for his deeds.—
We hung him up dry before just heaven's eye
   To throttle the imbecile's creeds.

But tell me, I beg of you, why you so speak
   As *Northerners* over him rant,
When *Southerners* aid, with both money and spade,
   The Yankee a monument plant!

Aye, plant it—and also contribute a *fund*,
   And,—heaven forgive them!—the soil;
Once red with the flood of our heroes' own blood!
   May God such disloyalty foil.

Enough—I will finish this spasm of woe,
   And thank you for list'ning the while—
I fear to dispose of the usual prose,
   Will instigate you to revile.

The weather's delightful, and balmy and soft;—
   With signs of a premature spring;
And new Easter bonnets, spring poems and sonnets
   Such weathers infallible bring.

My wife and her "lord" never had better health;
   As far as good health really goes—
With now a slight sneeze as a grippe-laden breeze,
   Plays "hide-and-go-seek" in your nose.

March 21, 1895.

SATAN'S SONG.

I am fallen—yes I'm fallen
   From a high estate;
Out of heaven was I driven—
   'Twas a happy fate.

I am ruler— yes I'm ruler—
   Of the world of sin;
From a thraldom to a kingdom
   Was I driven in.

SATAN'S SONG.

I created—yes created—
 Hell, a world of groan;
And I reign amidst the pain,
 On a sable throne.

I am lord of—yes I'm lord of—
 All that murky world;
From my tower, breathing power,
 Waves my flag unfurled.

Ah, that banner—Hell's own banner—
 Spreads its inky folds;
And in mock'ry marks a vict'ry
 Over human souls.

And my breezes—fiery breezes—
 Play on parched lips;
Parched ever—ha, and never
 Cooling water sips.

O'er my domain, vast, eternal—
 Hangs a sombre gloom;
Thro' its portals hurled are mortals
 To eternal doom.

Fiends and demons—Hell-born demons
 Subject to my will;
Grin with rapture when they capture
 Souls my Hell to fill.

Imps, my servants—trusted servants—
 Grant the soul no rest;
Gloat o'er anguish—hope extinguish—
 In the doomed breast.

SATAN'S SONG.

I am King of—worshipped King of—
  Part that region,—earth ;
And I revel in fresh evil
  Born with every birth.

All that portion—hellish portion—
  With its sin is mine ;
God's own image bows in homage
  To his rival's shrine.

Ha, I'm master—solely master
  Of this sphere of crime;
Hovering pinions guard my minions
  For maturer time.

In the temples—holy places—
  Thro' those incensed aisles,
Do I wonder and grow fonder
  Of the priestly wiles.

Thro' those temples—to the arches—
  Swell the sacred notes.
From the choir, higher and higher
  Hymic cadence floats.

At the chancel, gilded chancel—
  Kneels the devotee ;
See him falter 'fore the altar
  Serving only me !

Ha, I'm King of—secret King of—
  All that saintly throng—
Pastor ranting ; people chanting
  Hypocritic song.

And I'm watching—only waiting—
  Thrilling with delight—
Rapture dreaming—joy a-gleaming—
  For eternal night.

MY POOR KITTEN.

Listen to my tale distressing;
  Of the sorrow laden time,
When within the family circle,
  I received that cat of mine.

It was but an infant kitten—
  Sleek of fur and silent tread;
With two eyes of mid-night burning
  Fiercely in that infant head.

Claws of but the usual number,
  Teeth projecting from each jaw,
Tail of just required dimensions
  "As provided by the law."

I distinctly still remember
  (Oh the horror haunted past)
Of a transformation which has
  O'er my soul its shadow cast.

That she did contract a mania—
  Many manias, I can swear—
That she lost her infant sweetness,
  I can solemnly declare.

MY POOR KITTEN.

That she parted with her manners,
  But her claws and cunning kept,
Was apparent as the day light—
  And I swear she never slept.

How my heart within me sinketh,
  When that vision I recall—
As I see her climb the casement
  And straight out the window fall.

Oh the sorrow-tinted mem'ry
  Of the horror-haunted night
When some neighbor had accepted
  Invitations for a fight.

She had grown in vice and knav'ry—
  But her brains forgot to grow.
She was fool and knave together
  With a countenance of woe.

Oh the placid smile of weakness—
  Oh, the look of gentle hope
That she wore when once I fished her,
  From a pot of boiling soap.

Oh, my poor ill-fated kitten;
  In my dreams I see you yet,
Struggling with the little water—
  In my cistern, soaking wet.

Friends, you never saw a kitten—
  (Please excuse this childish grief)
That was so especially fond of
  Choice and tender breakfast beef.

MY POOR KITTEN.

Thro' the house one day she wandered
 In the cheerfulness of sin—
Wandered to refrigerator—
 Cook unknowing—shut her in.

On the shelves of groc'ries laden
 Paced that idiotic cat—
And when finished all the courses,
 In the jar of butter sat.

Twenty pounds of ice for company,
 Tail and moments both to drag ;
There I found her in the morning,
 Looking like a frozen rag.

Oh, the recollections of her,
 Haunt me like a troubled dream,
As I see her blandly wading
 Through a dish of cherished cream.

On the subject of digestion,
 She could give the ostrich points,
One good avalanche of victuals
 Only loosened up her joints.

On a silent sultry Sunday,
 Once her form was lost to view ;
When detecting foreign fragrance,
 Found her bathing in the stew.

She was destined ne'er to flourish,
 This my poor unlucky cat ;
One ill-natured kettle mashed her,
 Flatter than a table mat.

Oh, those mute appeals for pardon,
  Riseth still to mem'ry greet,
When in coping with the darkness,
  She'd get tangled in your feet.

Oh the mournful train of memories,
  Coupled with that tragic scene :—
When she had in blissful folly
  Drunk the can of kerosene.

And with appetite increasing,
  Innocent of pending fate,
Pounced upon a fatal relish,
  Twenty heads of matches ate.

From this mortal combination,
  Death had claimed her as I feared,
And a cloud has o'er me settled,
  Since my kitten disappeared.

JOHN DOODLE'S NEW YEAR RESOLUTIONS.

Presenting a familiar fact in connection therewith, sustained by two-thirds of mankind.

John Doodle was a fickle man,
  A human weather-vane ;
Susceptible to moral shifts
  No mortal could maintain.

JOHN DOODLE'S NEW YEAR RESOLUTIONS

John Doodle had a deadly foe—
 A rival motive force,
Which did decoy his falt'ring moods
 From their uncertain source.

John Doodle deemed it fit and wise,
 To formulate a plan
To vanquish quite this knight of ill,
 He dubbed Sir Other-man.

And thus he met th' infant year
 In calculating humor;
Quoth he: "I'll crush this demagogue—
 And gossip eat the rumor."

He fell upon the hardened knave
 In moralizing manner;
And flayed in fashion most approved.
 Like some accomplished tanner.

Again quoth he: "My honored Sir,
 Your comp'ny I renounce;
This day I resolutions make,
 And publicly announce.

You are the most abandoned rogue
 That ever chased the devil;
You wove a net of social snares
 That tangled me in evil."

Sir Other-man with smiles replied:
 "Reflect upon this measure;
Instinctive nature's appetite
 Demands a little pleasure."

JOHN DOODLE'S NEW YEAR RESOLUTIONS.

But O John did repel the tones
  That charmed his guardian spirit;
On "Zion's Ship" he chronicled
  Some pledges made to cheer it.

"And now my sin-dyed rioter,
  Please note our situation;
Should Folly beg you mediate,
  Suppress th' invitation."

Sir Other-man did only smile:
  "Reflect upon this measure;
Instinctive nature's appetite
  Demands a little pleasure."

John Doodle was a thoughful man,
  And prone to self-debating;
He credited opposing strength,
  And gave it honest rating.

So thus he deigned a grave response:
  "My gay, loquacious charmer,
The serpent may not catch Miss Bird,
  But still he does alarm her.

Your logic breathes convincing air,
  I grant, though 'gainst my feeling—
Conceding only to defend
  My claims of honest dealing."

Sir Knight was heard to murmur low:
  "Reflect upon this measure;
Instinctive natures's appetite
  Demands a little pleasure."

JOHN DOODLE'S NEW YEAR RESOLUTIONS.

By dint of search it doth appear,
   John Doodle's rage diminished ;
The tempest of his vowed intents
   In fluctuations finished.

Desire bred to palliate,
   Encouraged John to ponder ;
Abetting doubts unchained his mind,
   And let his scruples wander.

"Sir Champion gay I tender you
   A merited laudation ;
So sober an array of facts,
   Persuades my commendation."

(Sir Other-man on vantage-ground)
   "Reflect upon this measure ;
Instinctive nature's appetite
   Demands a little pleasure."

This truth evolved from Adam's fall,
   With suddenness possessed him ;
Collat'ral absolution, next,
   Immediately impressed him.

Sir Other-man the victory won ;
   Let no exhorter wonder—
Much stronger cords of firm resolve
   Are often torn asunder.

John Doodle now in merry mood,
   Exclaims : "This is relieving—
My gallant comrade, pardon me,
   I've been a-you deceiving."

TO A MATCH.

After an attempt to strike one in the dark, with the result of breaking it in two.

Oh sulphur wretch,
I came to fetch
Thy aid against defiant embers;
But curse thy head,
Thy virtue's fled;
And left thee in disjointed members.

I do believe,
That to deceive
Your seed advanced to wooden manhood;
And now you lie,
Content to die,
Sustaining thy reputed fiendhood.

Thy grain was crossed,
Thy value lost,
Before thy top with fire was christened
But with thy head
Bedecked in red,
In conscious deviltry you glistened.

Consoling thought,
This plight has brought
A fatal vent to lurking knavery.
For years you wore—
For years you bore
A look so meek 'twas actual slavery.

Indeed it's sad,
To think you had
Perspective schemes 'gainst tender fingers;
But priceless boon,
Death came too soon—
Thy spite in hated mem'ry lingers.

TO ———
Written for John B. Austin.

Just shake a mountain from its base—
Conceive the De'il returned to grace—
Exhort the world to pious turn—
Or any good from evil learn.
Then brand my love a fickle flame,
Just pass the word—forget my name.
But *not* until this comes to pass,
Declare such verdict sweetest lass.
In this retreat, within each line,
A heart is hid who'd life resign
At thy command, my Valentine.

KEY: Take first letter first line; second letter second line; third letter third line, and so on to end.

A STANZA.
Written on the Front Door of a house in Duluth, Minn., on vacating it, January 12, 1895.

Should 'gainst his foe a man desire,
His hatred to appease;
Just put him in this damned house—
To death he'd surely freeze.

IMPRESSIONS.

I watch by night the roaming star
    The lures to worlds enchanted ;
And grieve to see my nightly guide
    By gathering light supplanted.
I sink beneath awak'ning dreams,
    The joys I fondly cherished ;
That lulled me in the silent night,
    And in the morning perished.

I feel the chill approach of dawn
    That lowers on the morrow ;
And bitterly resume my way
    In solitary sorrow.
I drift where'er my fancy flows,
    Beguiled by gleams of gladness ;
I sigh to crush alluring hopes—
    And bear a heart of sadness.

Realities benumb the soul,
    Obscure impulsive splendor ;
Yet to a sovereign law we still,
    Reluctant homage render.
I yield release to social cheer,
    Ambitions stirred to languish ;
I mourn because the charms of night
    Are chained to days of anguish.

ON THE DEATH OF OLIVER WENDELL HOLMES.

He's gone, gone to eternal rest;
  The requiem song is sung;—
    They've tolled the bell—
    His funeral knell
In slow and solemn peals was rung.

No more his sweet, serenest smiles,
  Their matchless lustre shed;
    His hallowed soul
    Has reached its goal—
Through heaven's golden portals fled.

Deep sorrow holds the nation's heart,
  And sadness spreads her pall;
    The silent tomb—
    In ghostly gloom,—
One more engulfs within its wall.

The autumn winds, in yellow track,
  Blew forth a soul to free;
    A blighting breath
    From chilly death—
"The last leaf" fell from off the tree.

So Holmes has gone; the world will mourn;
  The "old school's" halls are dim;
    No one is there,
    For who would dare
Attempt to take the place of him?

The poet's dead—the wit has gone;
  His fame will ever stay—
    Such wholesome mirth
    Has blessed th' earth ;
Immortal in the " One-Hoss Shay."

Another spirit joins the throng ;
  And freed from mortal's pain,
    Has winged its flight
    To starry height :—
New England's loss is heaven's gain.

AN ENIGMATICAL VALENTINE.

Many lines are scribbled oft in vain
By those who strive to dizzy heights attain.
'Tis thus, when soaring high for fame, they fall ;
Their sudden turns, their puny minds appall.
Now is there reason for such hapless plight?
This it is, no *purpose* guides their flight.
Purpose should pervade each word and line—
Remember this and scan this valentine.
Here lies concealed from every curs'ry glance,
A name well loved by many. If perchance
A careful search this secret will unfold,
It will to you reveal what these lines hold.
But search—I leave the secret yet untold.

   Key—Take first letter of first line, second letter of second line, third letter of third line, and so on to end.

LINES ON A CORPSE.

Dull and cold, inanimate, lifeless thing,
'Tis at your weakness now I gaze affright
And shudder, wondering if thy estate
Shall be always thus. God's image true
Thou art, for so 'tis said—we take it so
Because we know no otherwise, and too,
Because the heart that in this lifeless clay
Doth lie asleep, once beat at a command.
We know that thou art not master of thyself,
For if 'twere so, the beating of this heart
Would start again by thy authority.
Thou art the essence of thy superior self,
With added weaknesses. Thou art an image
Of some superior thing—'tis reasoned right
That *It* itself eternal was, or formed
The nature of itself from empty nothing—
(Reason groundless 'cept we grant that nothing
Is its composition now—absurd!)
We argue;—from a model thou wert made;
It follows then that thou the essence art
Of that model; for at the first *It* was,
And only *It*—and hence thou art in part
Itself. So *It* is thy superior self—
It thy master is—thou art not,—
For thou controllest not thy vital's functions
In this thou yieldst to *It*—because 'tis *It*,
And only *It*, that's left.
Canst thou command the beating of thy heart,
With measured pace, to throw the life-blood thro'
This clay, as 'tis?

LINES ON A CORPSE.

Couldst thou the current of thy life-blood check
Or speed at thy disposal? Couldst thou the course
Of nature bridle, turn or thwart at will?
Why didst thou *die*? Awake and choose thy state!
Ah! thou art gone—thy compouent parts have flown
At the bidding of thy master—couldst thou them stay?
And thou dull clay art left from whence thou camst.
Thy *form* at first wert needed for an abode—
Material abode—thy finer self to hold
On earth—for think of *thought* itself alone!
But now thy mission is fulfilled, and thou
Return'st to Mother Earth, which art thyself.
Thy master calls the spirit which heeds his call.
But *who* art thy superior self and master?
'Tis every man's conception of his thought—
Interpretation of his yearning for
A higher state, dependent will, innate
In every breast—'tis this at which it stops,
And for no better name we call it God.

Oh! God is this the definite end of man,
Thy earthly self? Wilt thou recall thy breath
Always thus? Is man's allotted work
To be always measured by his death?
And shalt thou always summon death, thy slave,
To pluck from man, thy image, all that is
Thyself, and leave this earthly form for worms?
Is there no higher state for man on earth?

I gaze with horror on this corpse—a man
'Twas once, but now no more; a piece of clay
With pallid features, outlines of his mould.

Such stuff as that which potters mould in busts.
Oh sick'ning sight! And this the common goal
For which man struggles thro' his life to gain!
The flower buds—it blooms—is plucked—and so
Alike will always be man's destiny!
Man's born—the cup of life to his lips is raised
It tasteth good—but ere another sip,
Tis broken—then 'tis death, with poisoned wine,
Who serves the deadly draught, and man's no more!

TO MY PARENTS ON LEAVING HOME, 1894.

Kind hearts, farewell—grieve not for me;—
   And shed no tears—'tis best I go;
So yield—why not? by divine decree
   Tho' apart our lives, they onward flow,

As the struggling stream from mountain's height,
   Leaps and dashes on its way,
Nor sees another's mad'ning flight;
   Nor dreads its rush, nor fears delay;

But in a turb'lent monotone,
   Pursues its course thro' field and dell;
And with a hollow, muffled moan,
   It madly plunges o'er the fell;

TO MY PARENTS ON LEAVING HOME.

And onward, onward ever goes,
   Speeding, rushing o'er the lea;
Coursing, leaping, on it flows,
   To meet its brother in the sea.

Decree unwrit from Him above,
   Has sternly cut our lives apart;
But we can live yet linked in love,
   The tie that binds us heart to heart.

So we must wind, alike the stream,
   Our sinuous, sep'rate paths along,
To that dim vale Eternal-Dream,
   Where every echo is a song.

But as it must,—so let it, be—
   And by the mem'ries of the past,—
Each to each by affinity,
   We'll live forever in one at last.

And so weep not; we'll still be bound
   By that unknown, divine soul-essence
That has no name,—defies the sound,—
   And yet the pain of parting lessens.

Would that the minstrel's spirit of old,
   With spectre-hands would tune my lute;
Or swell with notes my empty soul;
   Or 'wake my muse, which now is mute.

Could I but hope, in some degree,
   With the poet's holy voice to sing:
This strangled heart would then be free,
   In boundless realms its flight to wing.

TO MY PARENTS ON LEAVING HOME.

But why rant thus? the spring is dry;
　The tuneless harp invites decay—
All natural things are born to die—
　So please accept this simple lay.

* 　 * 　 * 　 * 　 * 　 * 　 * 　 * 　 * 　 *

But pardon me for this digression;
　I know my song is senseless still,
But as I volunteer confession,
　Accept the deed, condemn the will.

And so we part to slowly drift
　Adown the fitful stream of life—
The right is ours, as yet, to lift
　Each fallen comrade in the strife.

We came, a home and hearth to seek;
　And open hearts we found and true;
Affection warm your acts bespeak;
　Kind arms, with love, around us drew.

You've done for us what sadly needs,
　A tongue more eloquent than mine,
To pay a tribute to the deeds
　Impelled by love, the spark divine.

And doubly kind you've been to me,
　As parents you have been to one
I love; to that extent that she
　Dominion o'er my heart has won.

TO MY PARENTS ON LEAVING HOME.

As solace in your smiles we found,
   Deep gratitude would stir our hearts;
But silence gave our hearts no sound,
   Yet spoke a depth no word imparts.

As 'round the festive board we sat,
   And offered up to God our grace,
We framed a prayer of thanks for that
   Which burst the clasp of want's embrace.

You gave,—we took—nor can regive:
   Except to trace on mem'ry's stone
With joyful tears,—engraved to live—
   Our love for you—our love alone.

A chance to meet life's gross demands
   You kindly gave for my reflection—
A thoughtful act, which now commands
   Me offer you my appreciation.

Enough—again kind souls adieu;
   'Tis best we go; we now depart,
And sacrifice a thought for you,
   Upon the altar of our heart.

We bid you all a fond farewell;
   Your faces dear will light our eyes,
And guide us, till at last we dwell,
   In "golden mansions in the skies."

TO GEORGIE.

LINES WRITTEN IN A COPY OF FATHER RYAN'S POEMS PRESENTED TO MY SISTER.

Could we but idly dream our life away;
Or either feel the touch of grace divine;
Could we but tune our hearts to sing or pray,
In golden cadence up to God's own shrine;

Could we but give our dreams a heavenly birth,
And heal the sting of life's ephemeral joys;
Then far above this dull prosaic earth,
We'd need no lines an age of time destroys.

Alas! the empty mockery of our life
Affords our heart's desires no purer climes;
So, to beguile the weary hours of strife,
We, sister dear, present you with these rhymes.

TO GEORGIE.

O, Georgie, they say (but Oh, pardon, I pray)
  That Cupid a conquest has made;
Your heart is a slave to this pitiless knave—
  His agent, a Huntersville maid.

O, Georgie, they tell how you 're under the spell
  Of blandishments sweetly array'd;
How oft in a trance you are thrown by a glance
  From the eyes of this Huntersville maid.

TO GEORGIE.

They tell me again of the actual pain
    They see on your visage portray'd
When some oversight has prevented that night
    Your seeing your Huntersville maid.

Again they can trace (so they say) on your face,
    A smile that has probably staid
Since last you have seen this unparalleled queen—
    Your sweet little Huntersville maid.

Come, Georgie, confide, if when by her side
    Your stamm'rings of love are repaid,
Come answer me true, are they brown, black or blue
    Those eyes of your Huntersville maid?

Come, Georgie, admit that 'tis heaven to sit,
    And watch the illumining shade
From downcast eyes, as when over it flies
    The smile of your Huntersville maid.

And tell of the fears that accompany tears,
    When love for second has strayed;
Then Oh, for a knife to annihilate life—
    "Farewell to my Huntersville maid."

This tragical act doth exhibit no tact,
    For when in the morgue you are laid,
She'll laugh you to scorn; and some creature forlorn
    Will capture your Huntersville maid.

Remember, my boy, the commodity—joy,
    Should ever be thoroughly weighed;
For anger oft slips thro' such cherubim lips,
    As those of your Huntersville maid.

TO GEORGIE.

Now, Georgie, the dart in a love-stricken heart
   Will surely the symptoms parade;
So do not secret all the tokens so sweet,
   But acknowledge your Huntersville maid.

Now open your heart and your secret impart;
   Of my confidence be not afraid.
Unburden your breast for I think you are blest
   By having a Huntersville maid.

Now Georgie, don't blush (if you say so, I'll hush)
   Your fortunes before her you've laid?
What, *no*? you forbear? then most truly I swear,
   You love not your Huntersville maid.

Should her you *adore*, you would waver no more;
   You'd make on this fortress a raid,
Proclaiming her praise, you would strike for a "raise,
   Then win your sweet Huntersville maid.

No doubt, I suppose, that divine little nose,
   Was shaped by angelical aid;
That seraphim wear the exact shade of hair;
   As that of your Huntersville maid.

I guess you are right, she's a fairy, a sprite,
   I trust when your fears are allay'd,
You'll rise from the shrine of this damsel divine,
   Demanding your Huntersville maid.

   Concluding—one word—you ask how I heard?
      Your *actions* your secret betrayed;
Your heart she doth ravage, your sweet little "Savage,"
   Your shy little Huntersville maid.

THE VALLEY OF REST.

The " Valley of Rest " is a shadowy land,
   Where spectral inhabitants dwell ;
And its borders are marked by a vapory rim
   Where anthems eternally swell.

Its waters lethean translucently flow,
   And eddy in silvery whirls—
And the moon-beams dance in a rapturous craze
   All over the garden of pearls.

A roseal fragrance nocturnally floats,
   Perfuming the tears of the night ;—
While the whispering leaves are perpetually bathed
   In a lachrymal vapor of white.

But the shadowy realms are all curtained from view,
   By a veil of aromatous haze ;
And the chorus of spirits flits noiselessly on
   In a whimsical, mystical maze.

TRUTH.

Endless toil and ceaseless strife,
   Without one ray of soothing joy ;—
Hate beget for the gift of life.
   And the sense of gratitude destroy.

NIGHT IN A GRAVEYARD.

Silence, silence all around,
    In the night;
And the solemn gloom,
Where the shadows loom—
Tenants of the tomb—
    By the light
Streaming on the ground—
Streaming from the moon, on the ground.

Death-watch ceaseless vigils keep.
    O'er a grave;
Here a stifled groan,
There a muffled moan,—
Spirits all alone.—
    How they rave,
From the hollow tomb,—
From the darkness of the hollow tomb.

See them, see them, in their shrouds!
    Funeral clothes;
Silently they tread,
Summoning the dead,—
Demons to be dread,
    In repose—
From the sounding vault—
From the dampness of the sounding vault.

MY OLD OWL.

My owl he sits and blinks and blinks
    With looks so keen and searching;
I can but stand and think and think
    How far that look is reaching.

Straight through my mind he seems to look,
    And then his head goes round and round;
He reads my thoughts like an open book,
    And then he blinks with blinks profound.

My owl he is a creature queer,
    A kind of evil-eye he bears;
I think he is a wicked seer,
    For such an om'nous glance he wears.

His glance askant doth make me shake;
    And then he leers with a knowing wink.
All wits at once my brain forsake:
    'Tis truth sincere, I can not think.

He looks and blinks, and blinks and winks;
    But from his perch he never flits;
It may be so,—he sits and thinks,
    While in monotony he sits.

I do not blush to own the truth,—
    I'm truly of this bird afraid;
And, too, I may confess, forsooth,
    My soul he fills with certain dread.

MY OLD OWL.

I often to him points propound;
    In answer comes his senseless hoot:
And at that weird and dismal sound,
    I stare at him in wonder mute.

I deem him wise beyond his sayings;
    His hoot, I hold his stock in speech;
I try to penetrate his ravings,—
    His store of wond'rous wisdom reach.

My mind, it yields in mild submission,
    To th' awful gaze of this bird of lore;
And though I make this meek confession,
    This state most truly I deplore.

Up in my throat my heart doth rise;
    And every muscle and fibre quiver;
I stand—seek vent to my surprise—
    'Tis vain—with terror cold I shiver.

The myst'ry that enshrouds this bird,
    I've often sought at solving;
For to my mind it seemed absurd,
    His look should reason start dissolving.

Now o'er this thing oft have I pondered;—
    Put this and that together well—
And then I sat and blankly wondered,
    If in this bird the devils dwell.

I've handled the puzzle well with care;
  I've turned the question o'er and o'er;
In my owl I find a wisdom rare,—
  The depths of which I'll ne'er explore.

My owl he's there a sitting still,
  The mystery I can not solve;
Tho' still a slave of his sweet will,
  My friend from blame I quite absolve.

MEMORY'S MISSION.

Backward memory speed thy flight;
  Stir up recollections dear;
Kindle as aurora's light;
  Ere departing, hark you! hear!

To those tongues of living fire,
  Not a mournful thought consign;
Liken not it to the pyre;
  Let the past their shades confine.

Summon not the vain regrets—
  Stings that youth from folly borrows.—
Mark you well how Time erects
  Monuments o'er myriad sorrows.

MEMORY'S MISSIONS.

Wake you not their deepened slumber
    Rest they 'neath the crumbling past;
Silent stones declare their number—
    Slacken not but leave them fast.

To the flames add all things pleasing,
    Make it as a beacon's light;
Fuel with love acquiescing,
    Till they leap to starry height.

With thy golden magic wand,
    Stir it to volcanic heat;
Let the blaze burn slowly down—
    Bring the ashes at thy feet.

*   *   *   *   *   *   *   *

Mem'ry hastens back at last,—
    Faithful mirrow of my mind—
Gazing at the treasured past,
    Pain, I see, is left behind.

Now my mind is full and clear;
    Memory her work did well;
Recollections see I here,
    Joyfully on which all dwell.

TO DULUTH.

Duluth, thou peerless queen of the Northwest;
Thy blushing cheeks caressed by zephyr's breath,
Defiance proud writ on thy noble brow,
Doth justly mock, in righteous scorn, the schemes
Bred by the red-tongued devil anarchy.
'Tis true, the finger tip of want hath touched
Thy shapely form ; but ere the demon reigned,
His ghostly, ghastly, unclean shape was crushed.
No murd'rous fiends hold sway within thy walls ;
No terror faces man upon his way.
Thy sons have ever trod on industry's path,
Thy rays of thrift o'er the country thou hast shed.
And tho' the nation's pulse did beat but low,
As when grim Want the land did stalk abroad—
Breeding discontent in the hearts of men—
Thy future pathway did but seem the brightest.
And, too, when sisters thine on every hand,
Crushed by the ruthless sway of gaunt Despair,
In piteous tones, their supplications made,
Thy coffers oped in quick responsive joy.
Thy eyes are oft bedimmed with happy tears ;
Thy soul is quickened with a jealous pride,
As Fame extends to thee her laurel wreath,
And o'er the country trumpets loud thy name.
Demanding commerce sends thy ships abroad;
Thy vaults abound with honest traffic's gains—
While science over thee her banner white
Unfurls, thy name resounds thro' the muses realms.

But be not e'en content with this, Duluth;
Let "onward" be thy watchword ever through
The misty veil of all the years to come.

PSALM XVIII.

(First six verses.)

O, Lord I will love thee—my rock and my strength—
Till the sand of mortality's trickled its length.
My God is my buckler; in him I will trust;
Salvation's assured from the enemy's thrust!

O Lord, who art grandeur, thy name shall be praised;
My arms, though a martyr's, to thee shall be raised.
Encompassed by death I shall not be afraid;
The shadowy boundary elicits no dread.

The cords of the wicked—the sorrows of hell—
So girdled my soul that I prostrated fell;
I cried unto God from the depth of distress—
The bonds of th' ungodly no longer oppress.

THE CLOCKS.

Tick, tick, slowly ticks,
The old timepiece 'gainst the wall;
   And the pendulum swings
   With each moment it brings,
As the old clock stands in the corner of the hall.
   And it ticks, ticks, ticks.

Tick, tick, slowly ticks,
The brazen faced in the prison;
   And the crim'nal in his cell,
   Slowly waits his death-knell,
As the hands go round with a kind of fiend derision,
   While it ticks, ticks, ticks.

Tick, tick, slowly ticks,
The old town-clock in the steeple;
   And from out of its iron throat
   Bellows forth the hollow note.
As the time it sends to the ears of all the people.
   And it ticks, ticks, ticks.

Tick, tick, slowly ticks,
The timid old clock in the school;
   And it marks the space of time,
   With a sort of measured chime;
And it seems to strike by a formulary rule.
   And it ticks, ticks, ticks.

Tick, tick, slowly ticks,
The quaint old piece on the farm;
  And it registers the day
  In a listless kind of way;
But its rough form gives an undisputed charm.
  With its tick, tick, tick.

Tick, tick, slowly ticks,
My little timepiece on the shelf;
  And the tiny arms revolve
  With a desp'rate mad resolve,
To keep in time—my merry little elf.
  And it ticks, ticks, ticks.

Tick, tick, they all go tick.
The devil's own imps they must be;
  For they dance and they grin,
  As the wheels of time they spin.—
Oh! they tick us on with a sort of fiendish glee.
  How they tick, tick, tick!

TO NORFOLK.

Dear old crooked, sea-girt city—
  Ancient Norfolk, fare the well;
In a bosom torn at parting,
  Memories of thy grandeur dwell.

TO NORFOLK.

List'ning to the harbor's temper—
    Crested billows, silvery white—
O'er me steals a soothing reverie,
    Through the anger of the night.

Yonder stands the old Cathedral,
    Loftly, solemn and sublime ;
Voices from the garnered ages
    Speak in music from thy chime.

Strolling through thy streets, O Norfolk
    Strolling 'neath the stars alone—
Echoes swell in rhythmic volume,
    From the silence of the stone.

Ivy-shield, green Saint Paul—all
    Reverence to this aged pile ;
Welcoming in measured cadence,
    Footsteps up thy hallowed aisle.

Moss-bound tombs and time-worn tablets—
    Pages from an history made,
Breathe a sacred stillness 'round thee,
    Deep'ning more thy solemn shade.

Breaking through the morning vapor,
    Dimly steals the autumn sun ;
Cheering honest hearts of labor,
    Ere the daily toil's begun.

TO NORFOLK.

Loit'ring through thy narrow windings
    Humble roofs my blessings share;
Sheltering 'neath their rugged surface,
    Brawn of might and friendship rare;

Struggling with the art of living—
    Striving 'gainst its cold recoil;
Wrinkled brows their radiant token
    Of a life of honest toil.

'Neath the oaks' protecting shadow,
    Stands the homestead calm, serene;
Faces at the window keeping
    Memories of its glory green.

Soothing moments! happy respite!
    Nightly o'er the bridge's side:
Weaving visions from the ripples
    On the bosom of the tide.

Shaded pavements, dingy alleys—
    Every corner, nook and lane—
Stretches in familiar fancy,
    Fading, leaves a mist of pain.

www.ingramcontent.com/pod-product-compliance
Lightning Source LLC
Chambersburg PA
CBHW020142170426
43199CB00010B/847